An illustrated introduction to

Shakespeare's FLOWERS

by Dr. Levi Fox

O.B.E., D.L., M.A., F.S.A.

Director of the Shakespeare Birthplace Trust

Away before me to sweet beds of flowers
TWELFTH NIGHT, I, I.

Jarrold Colour Publications, Norwich
in association with the Shakespeare Birthplace Trust
Stratford-upon-Avon

Here's flowers for you

Shakespeare, poet and dramatist, was by birth and instinct a countryman and the influence of his native Warwickshire reflects itself throughout his plays and sonnets. Innumerable passages provide evidence of his love and knowledge of flowers, plants and herbs, while his enchanting descriptions of pastoral scenes and the wonders of the changing seasons disclose an intimate acquaintance with gardens and the countryside.

His early environment clearly made a great impression. Both Shakespeare's parents came of farming families based in the country a few miles from his birthplace, Stratford-upon Avon, itself a little market town, closely linked with the surrounding countryside and situated in the very heart of England. The River Avon, alongside which the town had originated centuries before as a river-crossing settlement, divided the Arden woodland country to the north, the remains of ancient forest, from the open fields and pastures to the south.

It was in this setting that Shakespeare grew up and though he left Stratford to make his name and fortune in London, he never lost his affection for his native town and countryside. It was in land at Welcombe on rising ground looking across the river valley over which he must have often wandered as a boy that he invested his money earned as playwright and part owner of the Globe theatre; and he chose New Place at Stratford for his retirement, there to enjoy its orchard and garden 'circummured with brick'. Here also was a 'curious knotted garden', to use Signor Armado's description in *Love's Labour's Lost*, which – like the knott garden which can still be seen at New Place – conjures up a colourful picture of a posy-like mosaic with no two beds of the same flowers together:

> *In emerald tufts, flowers purple, blue and white;*
> *Like sapphire, pearl and rich embroidery.*
> (THE MERRY WIVES OF WINDSOR, V, 5.)

◄ *Primrose*

Shakespeare's knowledge of flowers was not that of a botanist or horticulturist but rather of a countryman gifted with an acute sense of observation which noted the colour, the form and the smell of particular flowers and plants. Moreover, he was capable of allowing his sensitive feelings to absorb their beauty and fragrance and then to use his matchless gift of poetry to describe their characteristics and through imagery to relate them to human life.

It is clear from his accurate descriptions that Shakespeare was familiar with all the wild and cultivated flowers of his time and the illustrations and references which follow suggest a keen awareness of the natural beauty and symbolism of individual plants. He seems to have been particularly fond of spring flowers, heralding the season

> *When proud pied April dress'd in all his trim*
> *Hath put a spirit of youth in everything*

This was the time

> *When daisies pied and violets blue*
> *And lady-smocks all silver-white,*
> *And cuckoo buds of yellow hue*
> *Do paint the meadows with delight.*

What more perfect word picture than this spring song at the end of *Love's Labour's Lost*?

Or what could excel his exquisite expression of love for natural scenes he knew so well as the fairy song of Oberon in *A Midsummer Night's Dream*:

> *. . . a bank whereon the wild thyme blows,*
> *Where oxlips and the nodding violet grows;*
> *Quite over-canopied with luscious woodbine,*
> *With sweet musk-roses, and with eglantine.*

Or his incomparable description of meadow flowers in *King Henry V*:

> *The even mead that erst brought sweetly forth*
> *The freckled cowslip, burnet and green clover.*

To the poet even the most common flowers in meadow, hedgerow and wood were full of meaning, no less than the birds and all other living things. He speaks with affection of 'those pretty flow'rets', of 'blossoms passing fair' and of 'the darling buds' of May. How aptly he portrays the characteristic features of individual flowers in an unforgettable single word or phrase: the

Lily

'pale' primrose, the 'nodding' violet, the 'bold' oxlips, the cuckoo-buds 'of yellow hue', the 'azur'd' harebell, the 'milk-white' rose and the 'winking' mary-buds, whose habit of opening at the bidding of the sun is described in *Cymbeline*:

> And winking mary-buds begin
> To ope their golden eyes;
> With everything that pretty is,
> My lady sweet arise;
> Arise, arise.

The lush freshness of the Avon meadows and the wooded landscape of the Arden forest – used by him for the romantic setting in *As You Like It* – clearly provided an almost magic inspiration for Shakespeare's poetic gift; but hardly less so than the gardens, both in his home town and in London, that he knew and loved. No fewer than twenty-nine scenes of his plays are set in gardens and orchards.

He was obviously fond of the knott garden, with its 'pleached bower, where honeysuckles, ripen'd by the sun, forbid to enter'. He depicted the beauty of the flower beds both at sunrise and moonlight, with the colour and fragrance of the rose, the pinks, marigolds and columbines, to mention only a few. He knew and understood the properties of herbs and the purposes for which they were employed. He was equally familiar with the trees and plants of the garden and orchard as of the woodland and hedgerow and he had an accurate knowledge of the processes of pruning and grafting.

In short, Shakespeare recalls the restful, old-fashioned loveliness of cultivated flowers in innumerable passages of his plays. No other writer has portrayed the atmosphere and character of Tudor gardens with such poetic feeling and sureness of touch or left behind such a rich legacy of floral imagery.

> Suppose the singing birds musicians,
> The graces whereon thou tread'st the present strew'd,
> The flowers fair ladies, and thy steps no more
> Than a delightful measure or a dance.

KING RICHARD II, I, 3.

ACONITE

The leaves and root of the Aconitum (common monk's hood or
wolfsbane) are poisonous and their deadly properties were likened by
Shakespeare to 'rash gunpowder' (*King Henry IV, Pt 2, IV, 4*). The
flowers grow in long spikes of a deep blue colour in early summer.

> *Though it do work as strong*
> *As aconitum*

KING HENRY IV, PT. II, IV, 4.

ADONIS FLOWER

The identity of the 'purple flower sprung up, chequer'd with white', described by Shakespeare in his love poem, *Venus and Adonis*, is not known for certain but it is probably the wood anemone or windflower which is commonly found in woodland in early spring and which withers quickly after flowering.

> *The flowers are sweet, their colours fresh and trim.*
>
> VENUS AND ADONIS

SWEET BRIAR
or EGLANTINE

The sweet briar or eglantine rose, which blossoms at midsummer, is a favourite in cottage gardens by reason of the fragrance of its leaves. It was described by Parkinson in his *Garden of Pleasant Flowers* (1629) as having 'exceeding large green shoots, armed with the cruellest sharpe and strong thornes, and thicker set than in any rose, either wilde or tame; the leaves are small, very greene, and sweet in smell, above the leaves of any other kind of rose'.

> *Quite over-canopied with luscious woodbine,*
> *With sweet musk-roses, and with eglantine . . .*
>
> A MIDSUMMER NIGHT'S DREAM, II, I.

> *The leaf of eglantine, whom not to slander,*
> *Outsweeten'd not thy breath . . .*
>
> CYMBELINE, IV, 2.

CUCKOO-BUDS
(BUTTERCUPS)

Buttercups 'of yellow hue' still clothe the green meadows of
Warwickshire with a carpet of brilliant gold in early spring. The
reflected light from their glossy petals gives the same impression of
unassuming beauty that inspired the poet to portray the cuckoo-buds
in such a delightful word picture.

> *When daisies pied, and violets blue,*
> *And lady-smocks all silver-white,*
> *And cuckoo-buds of yellow hue,*
> *Do paint the meadows with delight . . .*

LOVE'S LABOUR'S LOST, V, 2.

COLUMBINES

Like fennel, columbines were supposed to denote worthlessness or ingratitude, and it is significant that in *Hamlet* Shakespeare links them with rue, another plant emblematic of sorrow: The old bonnet-shaped columbine (hence the name 'Granny bonnet'), was found in woods but improved varieties are now popular in cottage gardens.

There's fennel for you, and columbines.
HAMLET, IV, 5.

I am that flower. . . .
. . . That columbine.
LOVE'S LABOUR'S LOST, V, 2.

COWSLIPS

Shakespeare invests the beauty of the cowslip, with its clusters of dainty, egg-yellow flowers, with a fairy charm. He uses the cowslip to indicate the size of his fairies – Ariel could lie 'in a cowslip's bell' – and compares the blemish on the left breast of the sleeping Imogen in *Cymbeline* to the 'crimson drops' in the eye of the flower. The 'freckled cowslip' blooms in early spring mostly in old pastures and on wayside verges.

Where the bee sucks, there suck I.
In a cowslip's bell I lie.
There I couch when owls do cry.
On the bat's back I do fly
After summer merrily.

THE TEMPEST, V, I.

The cowslips tall her pensioners be,
In their gold coats spots you see,
Those be rubies, fairy favours,
In those freckles live their savours.
I must go seek some dewdrops here,
And hang a pearl in every cowslip's ear.

A MIDSUMMER NIGHT'S DREAM, II, I.

CROWFLOWER

Although other identifications have been suggested, the crowflower was almost certainly the ragged robin which grows freely on marshy ground and blossoms from May to July. It has bright pink flowers with divided petals. In Shakespeare's time it was used in making garlands, so not surprisingly it was included in Ophelia's 'fantastic' garland.

There is a willow grows aslant the brook,
That shows his hoar leaves in the glassy stream;
There with fantastic garlands did she make
Of crowflowers, nettles, daisies, and long purples
That liberal shepherds give a grosser name.

HAMLET, IV, 7.

DAFFODILS

Shakespeare's exquisite lines referring to daffodils, spoken by Autolycus and Perdita, convey the beauty and freshness of spring in all its golden glory; to him daffodils also symbolised the joy and gladness of youth. Even the winds of March could not daunt the native daffodils which heralded the spring in woodland and meadow, long before the arrival of the swallow.

> *When daffoldils begin to peer,*
> *With hey, the doxy over the dale,*
> *Why then comes in the sweet o' the year;*
> *For the red blood reigns in the winter's pale.*
>
> THE WINTER'S TALE, IV, 3.

> *Daffodils, that come before the swallow dares, and take*
> *The winds of March with beauty . . .*
>
> THE WINTER'S TALE, IV, 4.

DAISIES

The daisy, one of the earliest flowers of spring so characteristic of the English countryside, formed part of Ophelia's garland in *Hamlet*. In *Cymbeline* the Roman captain ordered his men to 'find out the prettiest daisied plot' to make a grave for the dead youth, Cloten. The poet uses the simple innocence of this flower to convey impressions of grief and sadness.

The boy hath taught us manly duties. Let us
Find out the prettiest daisied plot we can,
And make him with our pikes and partisans
A grave.

CYMBELINE, IV, 2.

Without the bed her other fair hand was,
On the green coverlet, whose perfect white
Showed like an April daisy on the grass,
With pearly sweat resembling dew of night.

THE RAPE OF LUCRECE.

There's a daisy, I would give you
Some violets, but they wither'd all
When my father died . . .

HAMLET, IV, 5.

HAREBELL

Shakespeare's only mention of this flower occurs in *Cymbeline* when he describes it as 'azur'd' or light blue. It is a slender, bell-shaped flower found in woodlands and grassy banks. Different opinions regarding Shakespeare's harebell suggest it may be the 'bluebell' of Scotland or (as is more likely) the wild hyacinth of the English woodland.

> *Thou shalt not lack*
> *The flower that's like thy face, pale primrose; nor*
> *The azur'd harebell, like thy veins . . .*
>
> CYMBELINE, IV, 2.

HONEYSUCKLE

The fragrant honeysuckle or woodbine with pale yellow, or red and white blossoms, is a climber of vigorous habit, twisting its tendrils around shrubs and trees sometimes to a great height. In Elizabethan times it was often used to shade a bower or arbour. The name woodbine denotes its climbing character, while honeysuckle suggests the sweet juice of the flower and its juicy red fruits. Incidentally, the flower was regarded as an emblem of fidelity and affection.

> *And bid her steal into the pleached bower,*
> *Where honeysuckles, ripened by the sun,*
> *Forbid the sun to enter . . .*
>
> MUCH ADO ABOUT NOTHING, III, I.

> *So doth the woodbine, the sweet honeysuckle,*
> *Gently entwist . . .*
>
> A MIDSUMMER NIGHT'S DREAM, IV, I.

LADY-SMOCKS

The lady-smock, also called 'cuckoo-flower' because it blossoms when
the cuckoo comes in spring, is among the commonest of meadow
plants. In colour pale pink or lilac and occasionally white, its flowers
give the impression of a 'silver white' carpet when seen together in
sunlight in their natural meadow setting. It is this impression that
Shakespeare conveys in his exquisite word picture of the common wild
flowers of spring.

> *When daisies pied, and violets blue,*
> *And lady-smocks all silver-white,*
> *And cuckoo-buds of yellow hue,*
> *Do paint the meadows with delight . . .*

LOVE'S LABOUR'S LOST, V, 2.

LILIES

Together with the rose and the violet, the lily, of which there were several varieties in his day, was one of Shakespeare's favourite flowers. He uses it on several occasions in his plays and poems to symbolise whiteness or purity. To him it is an emblem of the highest beauty, comparable with the brilliancy of gold and the matchless perfume of the violet. In his heraldic references the flower–de–luce, or yellow iris, is usually mentioned.

Lilies of all kinds,
The flower-de-luce being one.
                    THE WINTER'S TALE, IV, 4.

What sayst thou, my fair flower-de-
*   luce?*
                    KING HENRY V, V, 2.

Like the lily,
That once was mistress of the field, and
*   flourished . . .*
                    KING HENRY VIII, III, I.

Now by my maiden honour, yet as pure
As the unsullied lily . . .
                    LOVE'S LABOUR'S LOST, V, 2.

To gild refined gold, to paint the lily,
To throw a perfume on the violet . . .
Is wasteful, and ridiculous excess.
                    KING JOHN, IV, 2.

LONG PURPLES

There have been different opinions as to the identity of this flower.
Some favour the common purple orchis of the woods and meadows,
but it seems more likely that the wild arum or cuckoo-pint, with its
stout spike-like flower projecting upwards, more aptly conveys what
the poet had in mind. This species has large heart-shaped, purple-
spotted leaves. It is also called lords-and-ladies.

Of crow-flowers, daisies, and long purples
That liberal shepherds give a grosser name
But our cold maids do dead men's fingers call them.

HAMLET, IV, 7.

MARIGOLDS

Although it has been suggested that the marigold Shakespeare had in mind was the well-known garden marigold, it seems more likely that his 'winking marybuds', which open their 'golden eyes' at the bidding of the sun, were the buds of the marsh marigold or king-cup which flourishes on marshy ground and alongside streams. The deep gold of the clusters of 'chalic'd flowers' as affected by the sunlight suggested to him poetic imagery of matchless beauty.

The marigold, that goes to bed
  wi' the sun,
And with him rises, weeping.
  THE WINTER'S TALE, IV, 4.

And winking mary-buds begin
To ope their golden eyes.
  CYMBELINE, II, 3.

No, I will rob Tellus of her weed,
To strew thy green with flowers;
  the yellows, blues,
The purple violets, and marigolds,
Shall as a carpet hang upon thy
  grave,
While summer days doth last.
  PERICLES, IV, I.

Her eyes like marigolds had sheath'd their light.
And canopied in darkness sweetly lay.
Till they might open to adorn the day.
  THE RAPE OF LUCRECE.

OXLIPS

Shakespeare's reference to 'bold oxlips' suggests the tall, confident character of these primrose-coloured flowers which closely resemble the cowslip, though larger in size. The true species is not found in Warwickshire but several common varieties flourish in woods and pastures in spring.

> *I know a bank where the wild thyme blows,*
> *Where oxlips and the nodding violet grows,*
> *Quite over-canopied with lush woodbine,*
> *With sweet musk-roses, and with eglantine.*
> *There sleeps Titania sometime of the night,*
> *Lulled in these flowers with dances and delight.*
>
> A MIDSUMMER NIGHT'S DREAM, II, I.

PANSIES

Shakespeare's pansies were the small wild pansies, known also as heartsease, which grow freely throughout the spring and summer. The flowers vary in colour, being found purple, yellow and white, and sometimes in variegated mixture. Shakespeare also called them by the old Warwickshire name of 'love-in-idleness' and used them for his own magic love charm, 'Cupid's flower'. The modern garden varieties of pansy derive from this species.

And there is pansies, that's for thoughts.
HAMLET, IV, 5.

But see, while idly I stood looking on,
I found the effect of love-in-idleness.
THE TAMING OF THE SHREW, I, I.

Yet marked I where the bolt of
  Cupid fell.
It fell upon a little western flower;
Before, milk-white; now purple
  with love's wound,
And maidens call it, love-in-idleness.
A MIDSUMMER NIGHT'S DREAM, II, I.

PRIMROSES

To Shakespeare the primrose is the 'merry spring-time's harbinger' or the messenger heralding the joy of spring. It grows freely in woodland and on wayside banks. The poet's description of it as 'pale' and 'faint' suggests a sweetness and tenderness characteristic of the freshness of the countryside in spring. He also uses the flower as a symbol of chaste beauty, as in the touching scene in *Cymbeline* when Arviragus throws 'fairest flowers' on the tomb of Fidele and in particular 'the flower that's like thy face, pale primrose'.

And in the wood, where often you and I
Upon faint primrose-beds were wont to
lie . . .
  A MIDSUMMER NIGHT'S DREAM, I, I.

Pale primroses,
That die unmarried, ere they can behold
Bright Phoebus in his strength . . .
  THE WINTER'S TALE, IV, 4.

The violets, cowslips, and the prim-
roses,
Bear to my closet.
  CYMBELINE, I, 5.

Witness this primrose bank whereon I
lie,
These forceless flowers like sturdy trees
support me.
  VENUS AND ADONIS.

ROSES

Shakespeare mentions roses in his plays and sonnets more frequently than any other flower. To him they were clearly favourites, both for their unsurpassed beauty and incomparable fragrance; and some of his most exquisite poetry was inspired by them. Particular roses that can be identified are the rich-scented damask roses of red and white; the fragrant Provençal or cabbage rose; the wild dog rose (or canker rose) with its trailing briars and clusters of pinkish-white flowers which adorn the hedgerows in June, and with glowing scarlet hips in autumn; the musk-rose commonly used with honeysuckle and eglantine to provide overgrowth to shade arbours in gardens; and the white and red roses, emblems of the Houses of York and Lancaster.

What's in a name? That which we call a
*   rose*
By any other word would smell as sweet
*   . . .*

ROMEO AND JULIET, II, 2.

I'll say she looks as clear
As morning roses newly washed with
*   dew.*

THE TAMING OF THE SHREW, II, I.

Come sit thee down upon this flowery
*   bed*
While I thy amiable cheeks do coy,
And stick musk-roses in thy sleek
*   smooth head,*
And kiss thy fair large ears, my gentle
*   joy.*

A MIDSUMMER NIGHT'S DREAM, IV, I.

For women are as roses, whose fair
*   flower*
Being once displayed, doth fall that very
*   hour.*

TWELFTH NIGHT, II, 4.

VIOLETS

On no fewer than eighteen occasions Shakespeare refers to the violet in matchless poetic terms and imagery which portray every aspect of this modest tiny flower: its colour, sweet perfume, habit of growth – 'nodding' signifies bending or hanging down – and purposes for which it was employed. The wild, sweet-scented violet with its delicate flowers ranging in colour from blue-violet through purple to white grows profusely on shady hedge banks and is one of the first spring flowers to appear. The scentless common wood or dog violet also blooms profusely in similar places.

Violets dim,
But sweeter than the lids of Juno's eyes,
Or Cytherea's breath . . .
          THE WINTER'S TALE, IV, 4.

These blue-veined violets
whereupon we lean,
Never can blab, nor know not
what we mean.
          VENUS AND ADONIS.

That strain again – it had a dying fall.
O, it came o'er my ear, like the sweet sound
That breathes upon a bank of violets,
Stealing, and giving odour.
          TWELFTH NIGHT, I, I.

CROWN IMPERIAL

Shakespeare's single mention of the crown imperial occurs when
Perdita links it with 'bold oxlips'. It is particularly striking for its tall
leafy stalk crowned with a cluster of beautiful drooping flowers and it
blossoms in April.

> *Bold oxlips, and the crown imperial . . .*
>
> THE WINTER'S TALE, IV, 4.

CARNATIONS (GILLYVORS)

Carnations, also known as gillyvors or gillyflowers, were favourites in Shakespeare's time and according to Parkinson were 'the chiefest flowers of account in all our English gardens'. To Perdita they were flowers of midsummer, symbolic of middle-age, blooming before the season of 'trembling winter' or old age. The streaked or mixed coloured gillyvor was produced by cross pollination.

> *Sir, the year growing ancient,*
> *Not yet on summer's death, nor on the birth*
> *Of trembling winter, the fairest flowers o' th' season*
> *Are our carnations, and streaked gillyvors,*
> *Which some call nature's bastards.*
>
> *Then make your garden rich in gillyvors,*
> *And do not call them bastards.*

THE WINTER'S TALE, IV, 4.

Spotted Deadnettle

Herbs mentioned by Shakespeare

BALM (balsam)   *Melissa officinalis*
As sweet as balm, as soft as air, as gentle.
ANTONY AND CLEOPATRA, V, 2.

CAMOMILE   *Anthemis nobilis*
Though the camomile, the more it is trodden on the faster
it grows, yet youth, the more it is wasted the sooner it wears.
KING HENRY IV, PT. I, II, 4.

FENNEL   *Foeniculum vulgare*
There's fennel for you and columbines.
HAMLET, IV, 5.

GARLIC   *Allium*
And, most dear actors, eat no onions nor garlic, for we are
to utter sweet breath.
A MIDSUMMER NIGHT'S DREAM, IV, 2.

HYSSOP   *Hyssopus officinalis*
We will plant nettles or sow lettuce,
set hyssop and weed up thyme.
OTHELLO, I, 3.

LAVENDER   *Lavendula spica*

MINTS   *Mentha spicata*

SAVORY   *Satureia mentana*

MARJORAM *Origanum vulgare*
Here's flowers for you;
Hot lavender, mints, savory, marjoram.
THE WINTER'S TALE, IV, 4.

PARSLEY *Carum petroselinum*
I knew a wench married in an afternoon as she went to the
garden for parsley to stuff a rabbit.
THE TAMING OF THE SHREW, IV, 4.

ROSEMARY *Rosmarinus officinalis*
There's rosemary, that's for remembrance;
pray, love, remember . . .
HAMLET, IV, 5.

RUE *(herb o'grace o'Sundays), Ruta graveoleus*
Here she did fall a tear; here, in this place,
I'll set a bank of rue, sour herb of grace:
Rue, even for ruth, here shortly shall be seen,
In the remembrance of a weeping queen.
KING RICHARD II, III, 4.

SAFFRON *Crocus sativus*
I must have saffron to colour the warden pies.
THE WINTER'S TALE, IV, 3.

THYME *Thymus serpyllum*
I know a bank where the wild thyme blows . . .
A MIDSUMMER NIGHT'S DREAM, II, I.

WORMWOOD *Artemisia absinthium*
To weed this wormwood from your fruitful brain.
LOVE'S LABOUR'S LOST, V, 2.

Here's flowers for you

SHAKESPEARE'S MONUMENT in the chancel of Holy Trinity Church, Stratford-upon-Avon, bedecked with floral tributes on the poet's birthday, 23 April, which is also St George's Day.